YEAR 1

COMPREHENSION AND VOCABULARY

Victoria Hazell

Illustrated by
Janice Bowles

Back to Basics Comprehension and Vocabulary Year 1

Reprinted 2016, 2018, 2023

ISBN: 978 192524 339 0

Published by Pascal Press
PO Box 250
Glebe NSW 2037
www.pascalpress.com.au
contact@pascalpress.com.au

Author: Victoria Hazell
Publisher: Lynn Dickinson
Editors: Ruth Schultz & Vanessa Barker
Design and illustration: Janice Bowles
Cover design: Deb Snibson, MAPG
Printed by Wai Man Book Binding (China) Ltd.

Acknowledgements
The author is grateful to Blake Education for kindly granting permission to reproduce extracts and illustrations from the following books:

Page 12, Lisa Thompson, *What Filled the Spot*, Storylands, illustrated by Craig Smith and Lew Keilar, 2007, Blake Publishing.

Page 16, Lisa Thompson, *The Scariest Thing*, Storylands, illustrated by Ritva Voutila, 2008, Blake Publishing.

Page 18, Lisa Thompson, *Facing Fears*, Gigglers, illustrated by Cliff Watt, 2010, Blake Publishing.

Page 22, Lisa Thompson, *Noisy Jungle*, Storylands, illustrated by Ritva Voutila, 2008, Blake Publishing.

Page 30, Katy Pike, *Reptiles*, Go Facts, 2003, Blake Publishing.

Page 36, Susan Mansfield, *Polar Animals*, Go Facts, 2008, Blake Publishing.

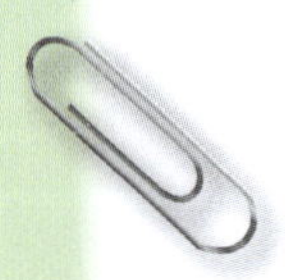

Contents & Checklist

ABOUT THIS BOOK

This book is designed to review essential Comprehension and Vocabulary skills required in Year 1. It provides detailed explanations of how to comprehend fiction and non-fiction texts in a literal, interpretive and applied manner. Each comprehension unit features a text extract with questions requiring literal, interpretive and applied comprehension of the text.

Literal comprehension:
What did the author tell you? Refer directly to the text to find the answers.

Interpretive comprehension:
What did the author intend you to understand? Read back over the text and think about what you can conclude from the facts you are given.

Applied comprehension:
*What do **you** think?* Relate what you have read to real-life situations and your existing knowledge of the world.

Parents or carers are encouraged to read the full explanations, on pages 8–9 for fiction and pages 24–25 for non-fiction, with their children before they do the practice units, and to discuss the glossary words under each text extract.

If further instruction is required, provide this book to the class teacher for review. A plan can then be devised between parent or carer and the school to ensure that all basic concepts are fully understood and consolidated.

Helpful features

- ★ **10 Top tips** are provided in full on pages 6 and 7 and are featured on the Practise pages. Read the tips carefully before reading them with your child, explaining any difficult words to ensure that each concept is fully understood.
- ★ **5 Vocabulary units** (Units 3, 7, 11, 15 and 19) feature activities using the 100 high-frequency words relevant to Year 1 students.
- ★ **5 Quick quizzes** (Units 4, 8, 12, 16 and 20) feature words used in the preceding stories and reinforce understanding of specific vocabulary found in the texts.
- ★ **100 High-frequency words** are provided in the centre of the book to be removed, laminated and cut out to make game cards for extra practice (see page 5).
- ★ **3 Tests** on pages 42–44, two comprehension tests and a high-frequency words test, are to be done on completion of all 20 units. These tests will check that the skills have been consolidated.
- ★ **BOB time! Back Of the Book.** At the end of most exercises, BOB will remind children to check the Answer section on pages 45–48 to make sure they are on the right track.

Ideas for using the Game Cards

The game cards in the centre of the book feature 100 high-frequency words that Year 1 children should be able to recognise, read and spell.

Two players

Player 1 flashes a card and Player 2 reads each word and spells it out accurately (without looking at the card).

Player 1 looks at a card and reads each word aloud (one at a time). Player 2 repeats the word and then writes it down. If a word is incorrectly spelled, take time to practise and then ask to be tested once more.

One player

1. Place all the same colour cards face down in a pile. Turn them over one at a time and read the words on the card.
2. Put the card face down on a second pile and quickly write down the words before you forget them.
3. Check that you have spelled them correctly and move on to the next card.
4. Score yourself and try to improve each time. Practise the misspelled words by writing them each five times.

Place all cards face up.
Sort into two piles:
Pile 1: Words I know
Pile 2: Words I am learning
Read aloud each word in Pile 2 and add them to Pile 1 when you know all the words on the card.

Australian Curriculum Year 1

Engage in conversations and discussions, using active listening behaviours, showing interest, and contributing ideas, information and questions (ACELY1656)

Read supportive texts using developing phrasing, fluency, contextual, semantic, grammatical and phonic knowledge and emerging text processing strategies, for example prediction, monitoring meaning and rereading (ACELY1659)

Use comprehension strategies to build literal and inferred meaning about key events, ideas and information in texts that they listen to, view and read by drawing on growing knowledge of context, text structures and language features (ACELY1660)

10 TOP TIPS

Helpful tips to gain full comprehension of a text

1

Main Idea

When we read, we can use features in the text to determine the main idea of the text. Looking for headings, bold print, pictures, captions and diagrams can help us work out what the text is mostly about.
So, look at the text and then ask:
"What is the main idea?"

2

Predictions

When we read, we think about what might happen next and make predictions based on what we know and what we have read so that we can find out the sequence of events.
So, read the text and then ask:
"What happens next?"

3

Cause and Effect

When we read, we can think about what caused something to happen and what the effect was. If you read a story or a newspaper article, it will always tell you what has happened and what caused it to happen.
So, read the text and then ask:
"What happened?" and
"What caused it to happen?"

4

Connections

When we read, we make connections between what we know, other things we have read and the text we are reading.
So, read the text and then ask:
"Does this remind me of something?"
"Is this situation like something that has happened to me?"

5

Inferences

When we read, we form our own ideas, or make inferences, about what we are reading. We can use clues in the text to figure out what else the author wants us to know.
So, read the text and then ask:
"What did the author want me to believe?"
"What was I supposed to find out?"

6

Monitoring

When we read, we should monitor our reading to make sure we understand what the author is saying, and have strategies to "fix" any comprehension problems as they arise. So, as you read the text, ask:

"Is this making sense?"
"Do I need to re-read?"
"Are there any text clues to help me fill in the missing information?"

7

Text Purpose

When we read, we should ask ourselves what the purpose of the text is. Did the author write to entertain the readers, to inform us about a particular topic, or to persuade the readers to think a certain way?
Read the text and then ask:
"What was the author's intention?"

8

Fact or Opinion?

When we read, we make judgements about what we are reading. We decide whether it is a fact or just an opinion and we should give reasons for our decision.
So, read the text and then ask:

"Is this a fact that can be proven?"
"Is this an opinion, someone's view?"

9

Visualising

When we read, we visualise what is happening while we read the text. Creating a movie in our minds helps us understand the setting, the characters and the events of the story.
So, read the text and then ask:

"Can I picture this new information?"
"What can I see, hear, smell or feel?"

10

Summarising

When we read, we summarise the information we are given.
To summarise, we identify the most important ideas in the text and explain them in our own words. So, read the text and then ask:

"What were the most important ideas?"

FICTION

Read together with an adult.

Learning to read is easy to do
It takes some work that is true
But when you can read a new world is found
With adventures and stories all around

Stories that tell of adventures and fun
Stories that tell of baddies on the run
Stories of creatures and mighty beasts
Stories of fairies and witches and feasts

Learning to read is easy to do
It takes some work that is true
Think of the places your mind will travel
Think of the mysteries your mind will unravel!

Remember: A reading coach could be a teacher, parent or other adult who can help you.

LITERAL COMPREHENSION

LITERAL COMPREHENSION

We understand what the text says. Understanding exactly what we have read is important so that we can then answer some questions about the text.

We can go back at any time to check what we understand.

We practise

What is the poem about?	Reading
What is the message?	Learning to read is work, but it is great when you can.
When you can read, what will happen?	Read all kinds of stories
What are two kinds of stories you could read?	Adventures, baddies on the run, creatures, mighty beasts, fairies, witches, or feasts.

Now that we understand what has been read, let's write a response in a full sentence using the questions ...

What is the poem about?	The poem is about working to learn to read.
What is the message?	The message is that learning to read is work, but it is great when you can.
When you can read, what will happen?	When you can read, you will be able to read all kinds of stories.
What are two kinds of stories you could read?	Two kinds of stories you could read are adventures and baddies on the run.

Do you agree with the answers? Check the text to make sure.

INTERPRETIVE COMPREHENSION

We understand what the text says and then link information or ideas together to get a greater meaning. We can then answer some more questions about the text.

We practise

In the poem, what does the author want people to do?

Learn to read.

We can interpret this because the text tells us *Learning to read is easy to do / It takes some work that is true / But when you can read a new world is found / With adventures and stories all around*. The author thinks people should learn to read because it is easy to do.

Why should you do what the author suggests?

You should do this because you will find a new world in the stories you read.

The text tells us *Think of the places your mind will travel / Think of the mysteries your mind will unravel!*

We can interpret this to mean that each story we read will have different settings and characters and different plots. That is why reading will always be fun, it will always entertain us, and there will always be a story that you will like. We can interpret this from reading the two lines of the poem.

Do you agree with the interpretations and the answers? Check the text to make sure.

We can go back at any time to confirm what we understand.

INTERPRETIVE COMPREHENSION

APPLIED COMPREHENSION

We understand the text, then add what we have learned to what we already know and draw conclusions. We will be able to answer questions that go **beyond** the text.

We practise

Read the poem again. Why should you learn to read?

I should learn to read because it is great entertainment – there are all types of stories for me to share and I will love them.

We can answer this question because we can use our knowledge and the words of the poem. We already know that stories and poems and films are wonderful, because we have seen and heard them. Now the text is telling us *Stories that tell of adventures and fun / Stories that tell of baddies on the run / Stories of creatures and mighty beasts / Stories of fairies and witches and feasts*. So we put what we know together with the text and we can answer the question. This is called using 'applied comprehension'.

Can you use what you already know to provide your own answers?

APPLIED COMPREHENSION

THE FIRST SCHOOL DAY

Read this with a grown-up and discuss any tricky words.

FICTION

Hooray! Hooray! Today is the day
That I go to school to learn and play
Friends I will meet, teachers will smile
The day will be happy and last a while

In the morning, some reading and some writing too
Then comes playtime with so much to do
There's cricket and running and games to play
We could be outside for all of our day

But the bell will ring and it's time to **return**
To the classroom inside where it's time to learn
This time **maths** is what it will be
Numbers and counting and **geometry**

We must try and try to learn all we can
About the people from another land
People from China, Japan and Pakistan
We must learn from them all that we can

We might learn another language too
It might be French, Chinese or **Urdu**
The language of music is another one too
And then there's art, it's a language, it's true!

So much to learn in the space of a day
There goes the bell, time has flown away
Home we all go with smiles on our faces
A wonderful day tomorrow awaits us

We practise

GLOSSARY

return	go back
maths	the study of numbers
geometry	lines, angles and surfaces of shapes
Urdu	national language of Pakistan

You practise

TOP TIP 1
What is the main idea?

 Where is the child going?

The child is going to ______________________________

 What is one kind of learning the child does in the morning?

____

 What might the child do at playtime?

____

 What will the children learn about after playtime?

____

 The children might learn about people from which countries?

____

 Why would this be interesting?

____

 What language might the children learn on their first day of school?

____

 Why might they be surprised to find out there are different languages?

____

 What must the children try to do when they are at school?

____

 How do the children feel about tomorrow?

____

BOB time!

WHAT FILLED THE SPOT?

Read this with a grown-up and discuss any tricky words.

FICTION

The sea star **munched** on the sea weed.

"Yum! That filled the spot," said the sea star.

The little fish **munched** on the sea star.

"Yum! That filled the spot," said the little fish.

The big fish **munched** on the little fish.

"Yum! That filled the spot," said the big fish.

The shark **munched** on the big fish.

"I'm still **hungry**," said the shark. He saw another big fish and **munched** on that too.

"Ouch!" cried the shark. A hook was **stuck** in his teeth. The shark was **angry**.

"I think I've got something," said the Captain.

"You've got me!" said the shark, snapping his teeth. "And you'd better watch out. I'm still **hungry**!"

The Captain and his crew **munched** on the shark with chips.

"Yum! That filled the spot," said the Captain and all his crew, and they headed home.

by Lisa Thompson *(extended)*

GLOSSARY

munched	to chew, to eat
hungry	to want food
stuck	not able to move
angry	to feel annoyed

You practise

TOP TIP 2
Predict what happens next.

1. What did the sea star munch?

   The sea star munched

2. What did the little fish munch?

3. What did the big fish munch?

4. What did the shark munch?

5. Why was the shark angry?

6. Why was the Captain pleased?

7. Why did the shark threaten the Captain?

8. Was the Captain scared of the shark?

9. Who won the battle – the shark or the Captain?

10. How can you tell who won?

BOB time!

VOCABULARY 1

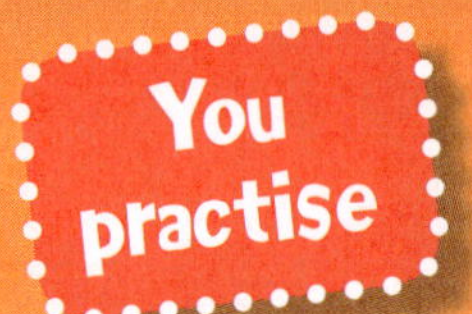

HIGH-FREQUENCY WORDS 1–20

The words featured in this unit are on the red word cards.

1 Words and meaning

For each word below, look at the shape, the sound blend and spelling. Read and trace over the word to make sure you can read it.

the	the	out	out
he	he	into	into
be	be	no	no
but	but	made	made
which	which	long	long

2 Pattern practice

Write each word, and then draw a frame around the word. This will help you see the word's shape and remember it.

of them for has this

make what over their little

BOB time!

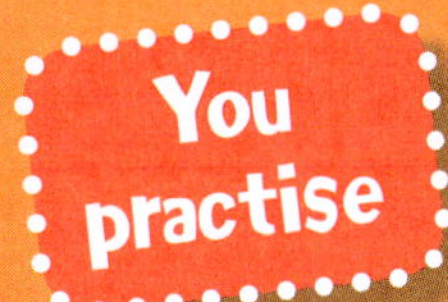

QUICK QUIZ 1

Unit 1 **The First School Day** Unit 2 **What Filled the Spot?**

1 Writing sentences

Write each word from the word bank in a sentence.

school	playtime	China	munched	hook
teacher	cricket	hungry	shark	angry

a I went to school for the first time last year, it was fun.

b ______

c ______

d ______

e ______

f ______

g ______

h ______

i ______

j ______

2 Jumbled words

Unjumble and write these mixed-up words from the word bank.

learn	fish	home	play	numbers
crew	captain	running	counting	reading

a incpata ______

b lapy ______

c rsbemun ______

d elran ______

e ninurgn ______

f nuocgnti ______

g wcer ______

h graedni ______

i meoh ______

j hifs ______

BOB time!

THE SCARIEST THING

Read this with a grown-up and discuss any tricky words.

FICTION

"I am the scariest thing on this island," roared Rex. His sharp teeth shone bright. "Nothing on this island is scarier than me." Rex stomped through the jungle. He roared his **fiercest roar**. He flashed his sharp and shiny teeth. Everyone ran as fast as they could to get out of his way.

Rex ran to the Great Lake. He roared his **fiercest roar** and he flashed his sharp and shiny teeth. Everyone raced out of the water as fast as they could.

Rex climbed to the top of the highest mountain. He roared his **fiercest roar** and flashed his sharp and shiny teeth. Every bird in every tree flew away as fast as it could.

Rex found a big cave at the end of the beach. He went inside. The cave was very cold, very wet and very dark.

Rex was not afraid. Rex roared his **fiercest roar**. He flashed his sharp and shiny teeth.

A roar came back that was twice as loud.Rex was stunned. He had **goose bumps**. The **roar** was twice as fierce and twice as loud.

Rex did not show his sharp and shiny teeth. Rex trembled. He had **goose bumps** on his **goose bumps**.

Rex turned and ran back out to the beach as fast as he could, leaving the dark, **damp**, **echoing** cave behind.

Rex was the scariest thing on the island.

Rex was so scary he even scared himself.

by Lisa Thompson (abridged)

GLOSSARY

fierce	scary	**damp**	wet
roar	shout	**echoing**	repeated sound
goose bumps	small lumps on skin, showing fear		

We practise

You practise

TOP TIP 3
Think about cause and effect.
What happened?
What caused it?

Why was Rex scary?

Rex was scary because ____________________

Where was the first place he went to scare other creatures?

____

What did the creatures do when Rex scared them?

____

What scared Rex?

____

Did Rex like to scare others?

____

Did Rex like the feeling of being scared?

____

What did Rex do when he was scared?

____

Do you think that Rex will keep scaring others?

____

Why do you think this?

____

Is there a lesson for children to learn by reading this story?

____

FACING FEARS

Read this with a grown-up and discuss any tricky words.

FICTION

Bruno stood **frozen** in the playground. A bee buzzing around and around him. Buzzzz. Buzzzz. Only Bruno's eyes moved, watching the bee. Bruno was afraid of bees.

Lots of his friends gathered around to **watch**, they knew he was scared of bees.

The bee weaved about, like it was studying Bruno. It got so close that Bruno could see the hairs on its legs. The bee stopped right before Bruno's eyes. Bruno's eyes were wide with fear. His heart was racing. The bee landed on Bruno's nose.

Bruno fainted.

When Bruno woke, the bee was gone.

"He's awake, give him some room," said Miss Fazio and helped Bruno to his feet.

Bruno felt his nose. "It didn't sting me!" he said, **amazed**.

"Maybe the bee was scared of you," said Holly.

"No, I'll bet it's gone back to tell the other bees at the **hive** how sweet you smell and will come back with its friends to sting you!" said Ned.

Bruno's legs went wobbly.

"That's enough Ned," said Miss Fazio. "Bruno, you are fine. The bee has gone and I am sure it will not be back. There is no need to be afraid of bees. They are wonderful **creatures**."

"They sting," said Bruno.

"Not all bees sting, and a bee will only sting you if it feels in danger. You should learn more about bees Bruno, then you won't be afraid of them anymore," said Miss Fazio.

by Lisa Thompson *(abridged)*

We practise

GLOSSARY

frozen	not able to move
watch	look at
amazed	to wonder
hive	house of bees
creatures	animals

You practise

TOP TIP 4
Make connections between what you read and what you know.

1. What was Bruno afraid of?

Bruno was afraid of ______________________

2. What did the bee do while Bruno watched it?

____

3. What surprised Bruno?

____

4. What did Ned say to tease Bruno?

____

5. What did Holly think of Bruno's fear of bees?

____

6. What did Miss Fazio think of Bruno's fear of bees?

____

7. Was Miss Fazio afraid of bees like Bruno? How do you know?

____

8. What did Miss Fazio suggest that Bruno do about his fear of bees?

____

9. Would Bruno still fear bees after he learned more about them?

____

10. Why should people learn more about what they fear?

____

VOCABULARY 2

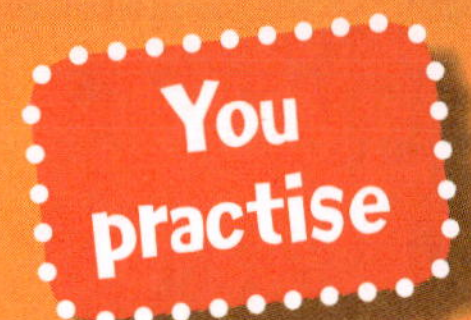

HIGH-FREQUENCY WORDS 21–40

The words featured in this unit are on the blue word cards.

and	said	did	I	her
was	then	very	were	first
from	more	a	if	down
all	than	on	she	after

1 String Words

Make string word by writing each one in a long string.
This reminds us what the word says and how it is spelled.

a him himhimhimhim ________________

b up ________________

c none ________________

d now ________________

e less ________________

f before ________________

g he ________________

h last ________________

i to ________________

j off ________________

2 Rainbow words

Write the ten words from the word bank, making each letter a different colour.

to	are	have	when	do
many	two	been	only	words

BOB time!

You practise

QUICK QUIZ 2

Unit 5 The Scariest Thing Unit 6 Facing Fears

Word grid

Circle each word from the word bank in the word grid below.

fierce	roar	damp	echoing	frozen
watch	amazed	hive	creature	fear

c	a	f	e	h	i	v	e
w	r	i	a	i	f	o	c
d	w	e	m	u	e	a	h
a	a	r	a	f	a	r	o
m	t	c	z	t	r	o	i
p	c	e	e	e	u	a	n
a	h	r	d	r	t	r	g
f	r	o	z	e	n	a	e

Fill the gaps

Fill in the blanks below using words from the word bank.

fierce	roar	echoing	frozen
watch	amazed	creature	fear

It was a dark and stormy night and a __________ wind blew outside. It was scary and I was __________ with __________. I was __________ that Mum was so brave. We heard a strange __________ outside the house. Mum went outside to see what sort of __________ could be making the noise. I could only __________ out of the window. Then I heard the noise again. This time it was __________ along the valley. Was the creature running away? What had happened? Was my mother safe? What had she done? Had there been a battle? Had she won or lost? How would I ever know if I did not go outside to see …

BOB time!

NOISY JUNGLE

Read this with a grown-up and discuss any tricky words.

FICTION

Pam was making some noise. She **hummed** and growled. Mark tried to be **noisier**. He shouted loudly. Pam made more noise. She banged and thumped on a drum. Mark tried to be even noisier. He howled loudly. Pam made more noise. She thumped and clanged on the pots and pans. Mark tried to be much noisier.

He **screeched** loudly. Pam made more noise. She **whistled** and screeched on her blow horn.

"Quiet!" roared Rex.

"Not another sound! It is time for both of you to be quiet."

Mark and Pam sat quietly in the tree house. They were both too scared to make a sound. They were so quiet they heard sounds they had never heard before. And they saw **creatures** they had never seen!

by Lisa Thompson *(abridged)*

GLOSSARY

hummed	sang with lips closed
growled	made a low deep sound
noisier	louder sound
screeched	high pitched sound
whistled	high sound made with lips circled and forcing breath through the hole
creatures	a living person or animal

We practise

You practise

TOP TIP 5
Use clues to infer what else the author is saying.

What did Pam bang and thump on?

Pam banged and thumped on ______________________

What did Pam do on her blow horn?

____

Who told Pam and Mark to be quiet?

____

What did Pam and Mark do when they were quiet?

____

Who was angry about the noise?

____

What action did Pam and Mark take after they were roared at?

____

What did Pam and Mark discover when they were quiet?

____

Was it important for Pam and Mark to be quiet?

____

Was Rex angry with Pam and Mark?

____

What is the message from the author?

____

BOB time!

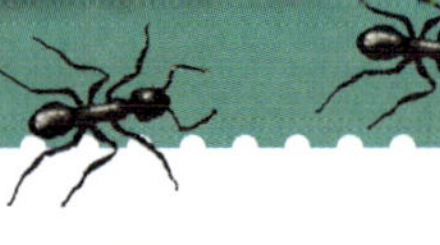

Challenging words to discuss prior to reading:
females colony soldiers

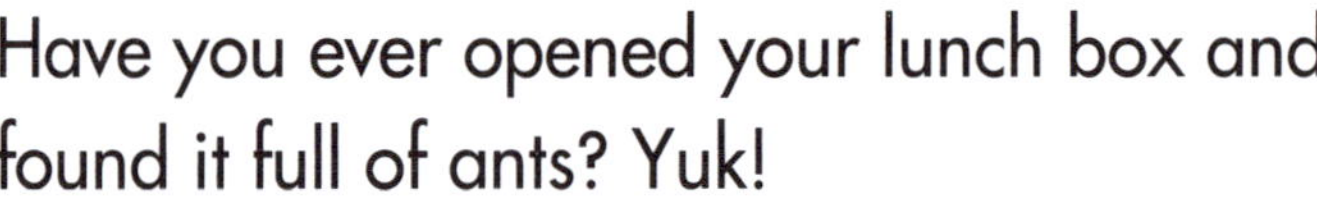

Ants

Have you ever opened your lunch box and found it full of ants? Yuk!

But there is a lot to love about ants. They are very clever, especially the females.

Ants live in a colony, which is like a team, and they all have a job to do. The queen lays the eggs. The female ants are the workers. They build the ant hill. They find the food. They are the soldiers. They carry the eggs away if there is an attack.

LITERAL COMPREHENSION

We understand what the text says. Understanding exactly what we have read is important so that we can then answer some questions about the text.

We can go back at any time to check what we understand.

Do male ants lay eggs?

Male ants do not lay eggs.

You practise

Do ants live in colonies?

Ants do live in colonies.

What jobs do female ants do?

Female ants build the ant hill, find food and are soldiers.

Do you agree with the answers? Check the text to make sure.

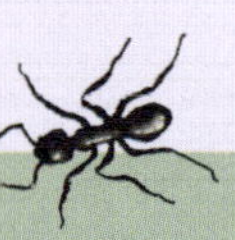

HIGH-FREQUENCY WORDS

YEAR 1

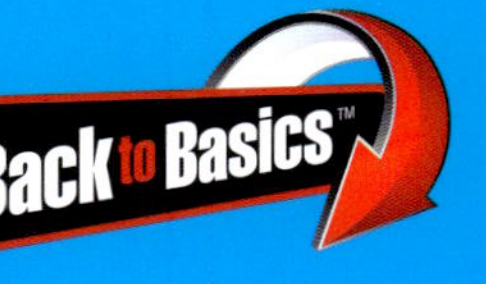

HIGH-FREQUENCY WORDS

YEAR 1

HIGH-FREQUENCY WORDS

YEAR 1

HIGH-FREQUENCY WORDS

YEAR 1

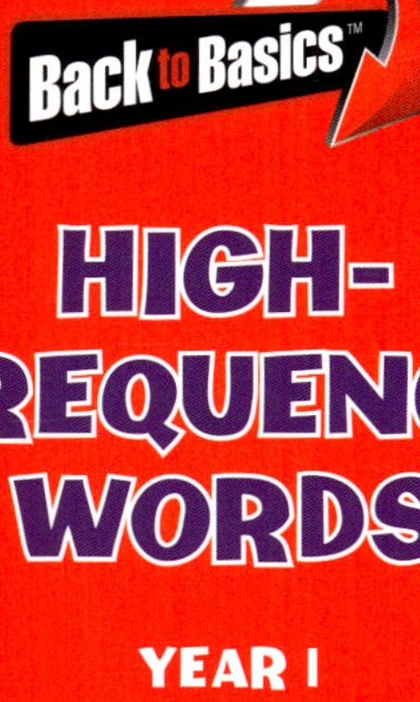

HIGH-FREQUENCY WORDS

YEAR 1

HIGH-FREQUENCY WORDS

YEAR 1

HIGH-FREQUENCY WORDS

YEAR 1

HIGH-FREQUENCY WORDS

YEAR 1

HIGH-FREQUENCY WORDS

YEAR 1

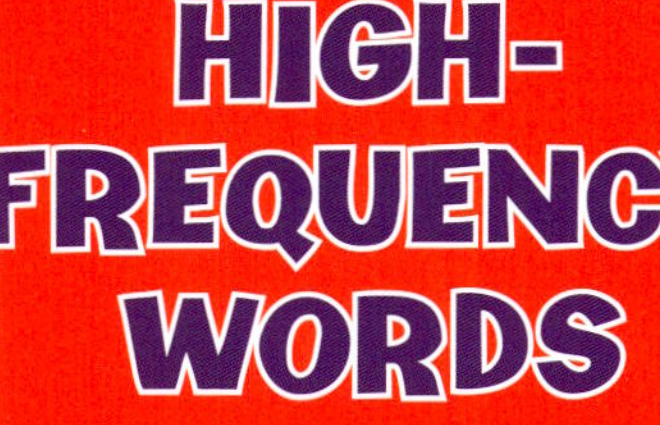

HIGH-FREQUENCY WORDS

YEAR 1

1 the
2 he
3 be
4 but
5 which

11 of
12 for
13 this
14 what
15 their

21 and
22 was
23 from
24 all
25 said

31 a
32 on
33 I
34 were
35 if

41 to
42 are
43 have
44 when
45 do

6 out
7 into
8 no
9 made
10 long

16 them
17 has
18 make
19 over
20 little

26 then
27 more
28 than
29 did
30 very

36 she
37 her
38 first
39 down
40 after

46 many
47 two
48 been
49 only
50 words

51	in	61	is	71	you	81	that	91	it
52	as	62	with	72	here	82	they	92	at
53	or	63	by	73	one	83	had	93	not
54	we	64	there	74	can	84	an	94	your
55	will	65	each	75	about	85	how	95	up
56	some	66	so	76	these	86	would	96	other
57	like	67	him	77	see	87	time	97	could
58	its	68	who	78	now	88	people	98	my
59	way	69	find	79	use	89	may	99	water
60	called	70	just	80	where	90	most	100	know

Back to Basics™

HIGH-FREQUENCY WORDS

YEAR 1

Back to Basics™
HIGH-FREQUENCY WORDS
YEAR 1

Back to Basics™
HIGH-FREQUENCY WORDS
YEAR 1

Back to Basics™
HIGH-FREQUENCY WORDS
YEAR 1

Back to Basics™
HIGH-FREQUENCY WORDS
YEAR 1

Back to Basics™
HIGH-FREQUENCY WORDS
YEAR 1

Back to Basics™
HIGH-FREQUENCY WORDS
YEAR 1

Back to Basics™
HIGH-FREQUENCY WORDS
YEAR 1

Back to Basics™
HIGH-FREQUENCY WORDS
YEAR 1

Back to Basics™
HIGH-FREQUENCY WORDS
YEAR 1

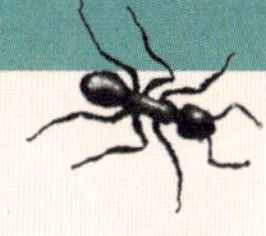

INTERPRETIVE COMPREHENSION

INTERPRETIVE COMPREHENSION

We understand what the text says and then link information or ideas together to get a greater meaning. We can then answer some more questions about the text.

Why would people think that female ants are clever?

People would think female ants are clever because they do the important jobs to look after everyone so they can all live, otherwise they would die.

We can interpret this because the text tells us *Ants live in a colony, which is like a team.*

What job would the queen have?

The queen would have the job of looking after the eggs and baby ants.

We can interpret this because the text tells us *The queen lays the eggs.* It also tells us what the other ants do, which is not looking after eggs or babies, so the queen must be the one to look after them.

Do you agree with the interpretations and the answers? Check the text to make sure.

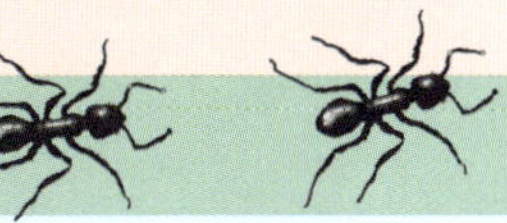

We can go back at any time to confirm what we understand.

APPLIED COMPREHENSION

APPLIED COMPREHENSION

We understand the text, then add what we have learned to what we already know and draw conclusions. We will be able to answer questions that go **beyond** the text.

Should people think ants are clever?

Yes, people should think ants are clever because they work as a team to build their own homes, find food, protect themselves and have babies and look after them.

The text tells us this and when we think about it all together, we can understand that this is how ants come to be in our lunch boxes! They are finding food to keep their team alive. If they bite us, it is because they are protecting their team. They are there while other ants are building their shelter. They are clever!

Can you use what you already know to provide your own answers?

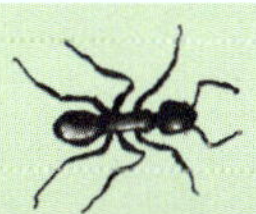

TYRANNOSAURUS REX

Read this with a grown-up and discuss any tricky words.

NON-FICTION

The Tyrannosaurus Rex is a **favourite dinosaur**. It is often in movies like **Jurassic** Park, Toy Story and Night at the **Museum**! Scientists think it was about 13 **metres** long and about 7 **tonnes** (that's 7000 kg). They looked very scary! They walked and ran on two legs.

Their legs were large and very strong. They had to be very strong because they had a lot of **weight** to carry! Their arms were quite small. But don't be tricked. They were very strong because they needed to hold on tight to their prey, so it did not get away. The Tyrannosaurus Rex had a very big head with very big teeth. It could easily crush the bones of its prey and other dinosaurs.

No wonder we see the Tyrannosaurus Rex in **scary** films!

GLOSSARY

favourite	like best
dinosaur	extinct reptile
Jurassic	time period
museum	place to display items of interest
metres	unit of measurement for length
tonnes	unit of measurement for weight
weight	how heavy
scary	to make afraid

You practise

TOP TIP 6
Monitor your reading to make sure you understand.

1 What is a favourite dinosaur among children and adults?

A favourite dinosaur is ______________________

2 Where are you likely to see a Tyrannosaurus Rex?

____

3 How long and how heavy is a Tyrannosaurus Rex?

____

4 Why were their legs so large and so strong?

____

5 Did they need large and strong arms? Why or why not?

____

6 Why did they have a big head and big teeth?

____

7 Why would other dinosaurs run away from the Tyrannosaurus Rex?

____

8 How did scientists find out about the Tyrannosaurus Rex's head and teeth?

____

9 Why don't we know everything about the Tyrannosaurus Rex?

____

10 Why are people interested in dinosaurs?

____

BOB time!

VOCABULARY 3

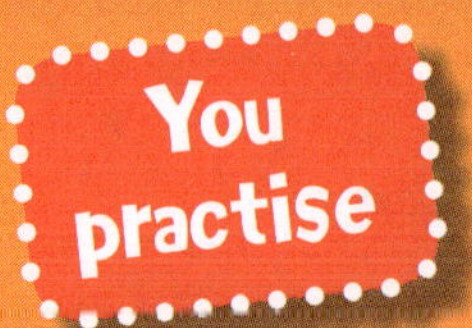

HIGH-FREQUENCY WORDS 41–60

The words featured in this unit are on the yellow word cards.

to	do	only	or	like
are	many	words	we	its
have	two	in	will	way
when	been	as	some	called

Back to Front

Write these backwards words the right way.
Read and remember what they say and how they are spelled.

a ot ____________________

b od ____________________

c ylno ____________________

d ekil ____________________

e era ____________________

f ynam ____________________

g sdrow ____________________

h ew ____________________

i sti ____________________

j ro ____________________

Look Say Cover Write Check

Look at each word until you are sure you can spell it.
Say it again and again until you are sure you know it.

a have

b in

c will

d way

e two

f when

g been

h as

i some

j called

BOB time!

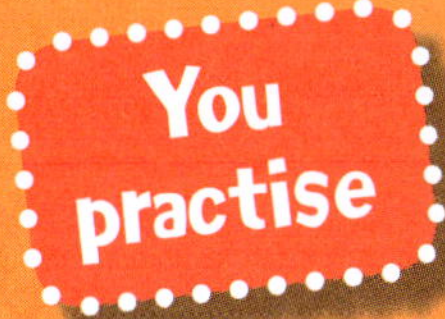

QUICK QUIZ 3

Unit 9 **Noisy Jungle** Unit 10 **Tyrannosaurus Rex**

Word meanings

Match each word to its meaning by drawing a line between them.

a screeched	noise made while lips kept together
b growled	sound made by blowing through lips
c hummed	high pitched squeal
d noisier	low, deep noise showing warning
e whistled	louder than another

2

Fill the gaps

Read the sentences and then fill in the gaps with a word from the word bank.

creatures Dinosaurs favourite Jurassic Museum

_____________ are the most interesting _____________ to have ever walked the Earth. My two _____________ movies are _____________ Park and Night at the _____________. They both have dinosaurs in them and they are both scary. The thing that I like the most about dinosaurs is that they were so large and scary. I cannot imagine being alive on the planet at the same time as they were alive.

I would be scared!

BOB time!

UNIT 13

A LIZARD'S DAY

Read this with a grown-up and discuss any tricky words.

NON-FICTION

How does a lizard spend the day?

1 Early Morning

At sunrise, the lizard moves slowly. It warms itself in the sun before going hunting.

2 Late Morning

The warm lizard can move quickly. Lizards **hunt** and catch **insects** and small animals.

3 Afternoon

After feeding, the lizard rests in the sun to **digest** its food.

4 Night

At night the lizard finds a **safe** place to sleep. During the night, the lizard's body cools down. In the morning the lizard will be slow moving.

Five Facts

1 Lizards smell by licking in the air.

2 Some lizards can drop off their tails to get away from **predators**.

3 Horned lizards can squirt blood from their eyes.

4 Most lizards have eye lids.

5 Lizards have cold blood.

by Katy Pike

GLOSSARY

We practise

hunt	search for food to kill and eat
insects	small animal that has 6 legs and often has wings
digest	the stomach turns food into a form that the body can use
safe	out of harm
predators	those trying to kill others for food

You practise

TOP TIP 7
What is the purpose of the text?

1. What are the four stages of a lizard's day?

The four stages are ______________________

2. What happens in the first stage?

____

3. What happens in the second stage?

____

4. What happens in the third stage and fourth stage?

____

5. When is a lizard most active?

____

6. When is a lizard most restful?

____

7. When the lizard hunts, why does it choose this time of day?

____

8. When a lizard has its biggest rest, why does it choose that time of day?

____

9. If you want to catch a lizard, what time of day would be best? Why?

____

10. Do you think a lizard must work hard to survive?

____

BOB time!

YOUR HEART

Read this with a grown-up and discuss any tricky words.

NON-FICTION

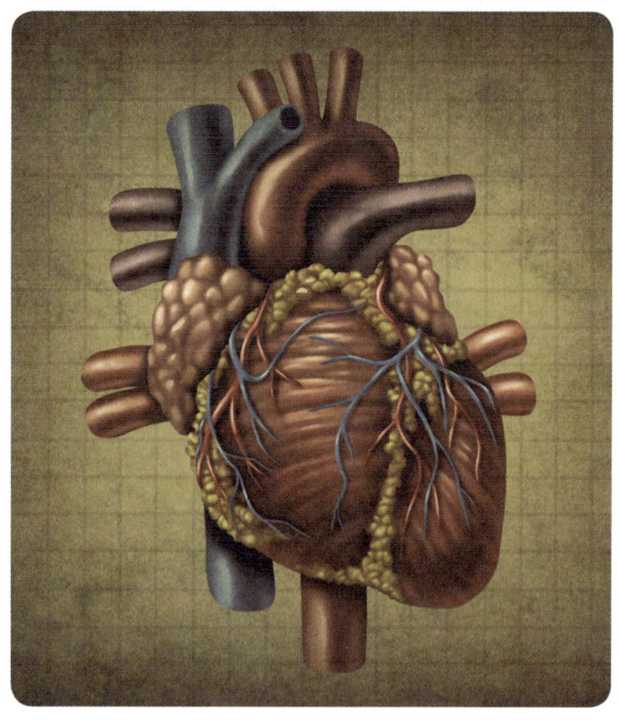

Your **heart** is your body's **engine**.

To make a car go, it needs an engine and **petrol**.

To make your body go, it needs a heart and blood.

Your heart works really hard. It works all day and all night.

It is a muscle that pumps blood all around your body.

The **blood** carries **oxygen** and **nutrients** to all the parts of your body to make them work.

Then it carries the blood that doesn't have oxygen and nutrients anymore back again to collect some more to deliver!

Isn't that clever?

Can you feel your heart beat? It beats about 100 times per minute.

Did you know?

Your heart is about the size of your fist.

Your heart sits behind your ribs, just to the left of the middle of your chest.

The '**lub-dub**' sound you can hear is the heart pushing blood out, then filling back up again.

GLOSSARY

heart	muscle that acts like a pump in the human body
engine	machine to run a car
petrol	liquid that will make an engine run
blood	red liquid that flows around the body
oxygen	a gas in the air that all animals need to breathe
nutrients	substances needed to live or grow
lub-dub	sound the heart makes

You practise

TOP TIP 8
Decide if what you've read is fact or opinion.

1 What word could be used to describe the heart for the body?

The heart could be described as ______________________

2 A car needs an engine and petrol to make it go. What does a body need?

____

3 What does the heart muscle do for the body?

____

4 What are two things our body needs to make it work?

____

5 Why does our heart beat faster when we exercise?

____

6 Why does our heart beat slower when we have finished exercising?

____

7 Why does our heart still need to work at night?

____

8 Why is the heart the most important body part?

____

9 Why does a doctor always listen to the sound of a person's heart?

____

10 Why is our heart behind our rib cage?

____

BOB time!

VOCABULARY 4

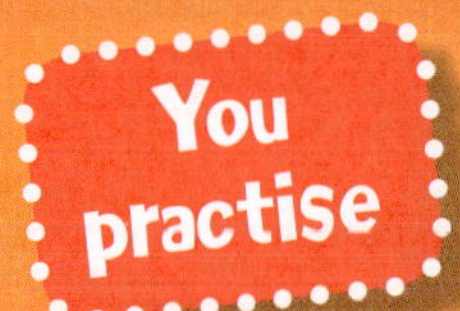

HIGH-FREQUENCY WORDS 61–80

The words featured in this unit are on the green word cards.

1 Colour in

by is with him there

find each who just so

2 Pyramids everywhere!

Make a pyramid for each of these high frequency words.
Spelling words over and over in our minds helps us memorise them.

you	one	about	see	use
here	can	these	now	where

a
a b
a b o
a b o u
a b o u t

y
_ _
_ _ _

o
_ _
_ _ _

s
_ _
_ _ _

u
_ _
_ _ _

h
_ _
_ _ _
_ _ _ _

c
_ _
_ _ _

t
_ _
_ _ _
_ _ _ _
_ _ _ _ _

n
_ _
_ _ _

w
_ _
_ _ _
_ _ _ _
_ _ _ _ _

BOB time!

QUICK QUIZ 4

Unit 13 **A Lizard's Day** Unit 14 **Your Heart**

Word snail

Create a word snail by writing these words into the snail's shell. Repeat the words until the shell is full.

predators hunt insects digest safe

Create a snail trail by adding these words to show where the snail has been.

heart blood oxygen nutrients insects

Going backwards

Write these backwards words the right way and use each word in a sentence.

a traeh ____________ ______________________________

b negyxo ____________ ______________________________

c doolb ____________ ______________________________

d stcesni ____________ ______________________________

e drazil ____________ ______________________________

f tnuh ____________ ______________________________

BOB time!

POLAR BEARS

Read this with a grown-up and discuss any tricky words.

NON-FICTION

Polar bears are the world's largest land **carnivores**.

They live on ice **floes** and the snow-covered land of the **Arctic**.

There are about 25 000 polar bears in the wild.

They are in danger because **global warming** is melting the Arctic ice. This makes it harder for the bears to hunt **prey** on the ice floes.

Polar bears have two layers of fur, and a thick layer of **blubber** which stops them feeling cold. Their white fur is good **camouflage**; it helps them blend in with the ice and snow.

Polar bears are fierce hunters. They mainly eat seals, but also birds, fish and even small whales.

Polar bears are excellent swimmers. They use their large paws like paddles.

by Susan Mansfield

GLOSSARY

carnivores	eat meat
floe	ice floating on the sea
Arctic	polar region in the north
global warming	rise in the average temperature of the Earth
prey	animal caught by another to be eaten
blubber	layer of fat around the body
camouflage	coloured to blend in with the environment, to hide

You practise

TOP TIP 9
Create visual images of what you read.

1 What are the world's largest carnivores?

The world's largest carnivores are ______________________

2 Where do polar bears live?

____

3 Why are polar bears in danger?

____

4 What protects polar bears from the cold?

____

5 What helps the polar bear when it is hunting prey?

____

6 What do polar bears eat?

____

7 What helps polar bears move through the water?

____

8 What feature do you think is the polar bear's best? Why?

____

9 Why is global warming bad for polar bears?

____

10 Do you think polar bears will become extinct?

____

BOB time!

UNIT 18

THE MOON

Read this with a grown-up and discuss any tricky words.

NON-FICTION

Would you like to visit? Here are some facts to help you decide.

The Moon is about 4½ billion years old.

The Moon orbits (goes around) the Earth every 27.3 days.

The Moon is very hot during the day: 107°C.

The Moon is very cold during the night: -153°C.

The Moon can look different.

If we **travelled** by **rocket** to the Moon, it would take about 13 hours.

The first man to land on the Moon was in 1969.

Gravity on the Moon is not as strong as on Earth. **Astronauts** have to wear special **suits** so they do not float away!

There is no air on the Moon.

There is no water on the Moon.

There is no life on the Moon.

Would you like to visit one day?

Crescent Moon

Quarter Moon

Full Moon

GLOSSARY

crescent a curved shape, wide in the middle and pointed at the ends

quarter one of four equal parts

travelled moved from one place to another

rocket vehicle like a tube that travels in space

gravity the force that causes objects to fall

astronaut someone who travels or works in space

suit set of clothes

You practise

TOP TIP 10
Summarise the most important ideas.

1. How old is the Moon?

The Moon is

2. How long does it take the Moon to go around the Earth?

3. Is the Moon hot during the day? How hot?

4. Is the Moon cold during the night? How cold?

5. How long was the journey for the first man to land on the Moon?

6. Why do astronauts need special suits on the Moon?

7. If you landed on the Moon, what is the first thing you would notice?

8. What is one way the Moon can look?

9. Why do you think humans are interested in landing on the Moon?

10. Would you like to visit the Moon one day? Why? Why not?

BOB time!

UNIT 19

VOCABULARY 5

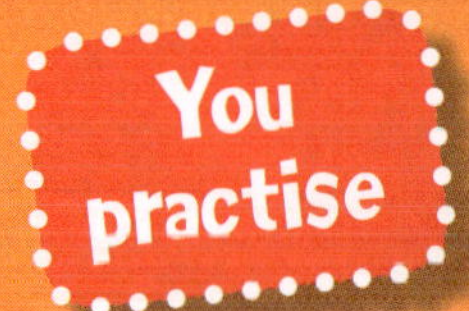

HIGH-FREQUENCY WORDS 81–100

The words featured in this unit are on the purple word cards.

Dotted words

Use a marker to create each word as a series of dots. Keep spelling the word over and over in your head so that you remember how to spell it.

that had how time may they an would people most

that

Grid me!

Use these words to create your own wonder word.

it at not your up other could my water know

1 Use a grey lead pencil and capital letters.
2 Write each word anywhere in the grid, vertically or horizontally.
3 Fill the grid with any letters of the alphabet.
4 Now use a highlight marker to find your list words!

BOB time!

You practise

QUICK QUIZ 5

Unit 17 **Polar Bears** Unit 18 **The Moon**

1

Interesting sentences

Write five sentences, each including two words from the word bank.

polar bears	prey	Moon	astronaut	rocket

a ______________________________

b ______________________________

c ______________________________

d ______________________________

e ______________________________

Word meanings

Draw lines to match the words with the correct meaning.

Word	Meaning
carnivores	vehicle to travel in space
Arctic	far north of the planet
prey	one of four parts
blubber	meat eating
camouflage	layer of fat
crescent	hunted to eat
quarter	coloured to blend in with the environment, to hide
rocket	person who travels in space
gravity	a curved shape, wide in the middle and pointed at the ends
astronaut	the force that causes objects to fall

BOB time!

TEST 1

FICTION: RESTRUCTURING THE TEXT

★ Turn back to Unit 9 on page 22 and re-read Noisy Jungle.
★ The text below is out of order. Put the paragraphs back in order by writing the paragraph numbers in the correct order in the boxes below.

☐ ☐ ☐ ☐ ☐

Noisy Jungle

1 Mark and Pam sat quietly in the tree house. They were both too scared to make a sound. They were so quiet they heard sounds they had never heard before. And they saw creatures they had never seen!

2 Pam was making some noise. She hummed and growled. Mark tried to be noisier. He shouted loudly.

3 Pam made more noise. She thumped and clanged on the pots and pans. Mark tried to be much noisier. He screeched loudly.

4 Pam made more noise. She banged and thumped on a drum. Mark tried to be even noisier. He howled loudly.

5 Pam made more noise. She whistled and screeched on her blow horn.

"Quiet!" roared Rex.

"Not another sound! It is time for both of you to be quiet."

BOB time!

TEST 2

NON-FICTION: RESTRUCTURING THE TEXT

★ Turn back to Unit 17 on page 36 and re-read Polar Bears.
★ The following text is out of sequence. Put the paragraphs back in order by writing the paragraph numbers in the correct order in the boxes below.

Polar Bears

1 Polar bears have two layers of fur, and a thick layer of blubber which stops them feeling cold. Their white fur is good camouflage; it helps them blend in with the ice and snow.

2 Polar bears are excellent swimmers. They use their large paws like paddles.

3 Polar bears are fierce hunters. They mainly eat seals, but also birds, fish and even small whales.

4 Polar bears are the world's largest land carnivores.
They live on ice floes and the snow-covered land of the Arctic.
There are about 25 000 polar bears in the wild.
They are in danger because global warming is melting the Arctic ice. This makes it harder for the bears to hunt prey on the ice floes.

BOB time!

HIGH-FREQUENCY WORDS

Ask an adult to read you the high-frequency words in blocks of 20 and write each word in its correct box. Start with the red cards (words 1–20), then the blue cards (words 21–40), the yellow cards (words 41–60), the green cards (words 61–80) and finally the purple cards (words 81–100).

1	21	41	61	81
2	22	42	62	82
3	23	43	63	83
4	24	44	64	84
5	25	45	65	85
6	26	46	66	86
7	27	47	67	87
8	28	48	68	88
9	29	49	69	89
10	30	50	70	90
11	31	51	71	91
12	32	52	72	92
13	33	53	73	93
14	34	54	74	94
14	35	55	75	95
16	36	56	76	96
17	37	57	77	97
18	38	58	78	98
19	39	59	79	99
20	40	60	80	100

ANSWERS

Unit 1 The First School Day

1. The child is going to go to school.
2. The child is going to learn reading and writing in the morning.
3. The children might play cricket, run or play other games at playtime. (Any of these is an acceptable answer)
4. After playtime, the children might learn about maths, numbers, counting or geometry. (Any of these is an acceptable answer)
5. The children might learn about people from China, Japan and Pakistan. (Any of these is an acceptable answer)
6. Answers may vary. The children might learn how life is different for people in other countries – this would be interesting to know.
7. The children might learn French, Chinese or Urdu.
8. The children might know that many people speak different languages, but they might be surprised to think of music and art as kinds of languages.
9. When they are at school, children must try to learn all that they can.
10. Answers may vary. They are happy because they have had a fun and interesting day and learned about many new things and they are looking forward to coming back tomorrow.

Unit 2 What Filled the Spot?

1. The sea star munched on the sea weed.
2. The little fish munched on the sea star.
3. The big fish munched on the little fish.
4. The shark munched on the big fish.
5. The shark was angry because the hook was stuck in his teeth.
6. The Captain was pleased because he had caught the shark.
7. The shark threatened the Captain, hoping that the Captain would let him go.
8. No, the Captain was not scared of the shark.
9. The Captain won the battle.
10. We know that the Captain won the battle because he and the crew ate shark and chips for dinner!

Unit 3 Vocabulary 1

Writing and reading practice.

Unit 4 Quick Quiz 1

Adult to review.

Unit 5 The Scariest Thing

1. Rex was scary because he roared, his sharp teeth shone bright and he stomped through the jungle. (Any of these is an acceptable answer)
2. The first place he went to scare other creatures was the jungle.
3. Rex roared his fiercest roar and flashed his sharp and shiny teeth and everyone ran to get out of his way.
4. Rex went into a cave and roared, and when his roar echoed back at him he scared himself!
5. Yes, Rex liked to scare others. That is why he kept doing it.
6. No, Rex did not like being scared. He trembled and he had goose bumps on his goose bumps!
7. Rex ran out of the cave back to the beach as fast as he could!
8. Answers may vary. Rex will not keep scaring others. Or, Rex will keep scaring others but he will not go back to the cave again.
9. Rex won't do this again because he now knows what it feels like to be scared, and he didn't like the feeling of goose bumps on his goose bumps.
10. Children learn that it does not feel nice to be scared, so they should never scare others. (This discussion could then transfer to feeling scared by others in the playground, how this can make others feel and why it is not acceptable.)

Unit 6 Facing Fears

1. Bruno was afraid of bees.
2. The bee buzzed around and around Bruno.
3. Bruno was surprised that after buzzing around him, the bee had not stung him.
4. Ned teased Bruno by telling him that the bee had probably gone to get his other bee friends and that they would come back and sting him because he smelled so sweet.
5. Holly thought that the bee might be scared of Bruno.
6. Miss Fazio thought that there was no need for Bruno to be scared of bees.
7. No, Miss Fazio was not afraid of bees like Bruno. We know this because she says that they are wonderful creatures.
8. Miss Fazio suggests that Bruno learns more about bees so that he won't be afraid of them any more.
9. Answers may vary. No, he would not be scared any more because he would know more about them and he would know they only sting when they think they are in danger. Yes, because he could still be fearful of a sting.
10. Answers may vary. People should learn more about what they fear so that they understand that the chance of danger to them is very small.

ANSWERS

Unit 7 Vocabulary 2

Adult to review.

Unit 8 Quick Quiz 2

1.

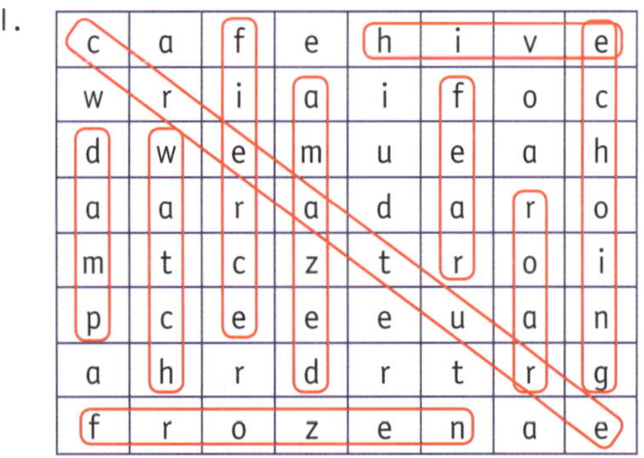

c	a	f	e	h	i	v	e
w	r	i	a	i	f	o	c
d	w	e	m	u	e	a	h
a	a	r	a	d	a	r	o
m	t	c	z	t	r	o	i
p	c	e	e	e	u	a	n
a	h	r	d	r	t	r	g
f	r	o	z	e	n	a	e

2. It was a dark and stormy night and a **fierce** wind blew outside. It was scary and I was **frozen** with **fear**. I was amazed that Mum was so brave. We heard a strange **roar** outside the house. Mum went outside to see what sort of **creature** could be making the noise. I could only **watch** out of the window. Then I heard the noise again. This time it was **echoing** along the valley. Was the creature running away? What had happened? Was my mother safe? What had she done? Had there been a battle? Had she won or lost? How would I ever know if I did not go outside to see ...

Unit 9 Noisy Jungle

1. Pam banged and thumped on a drum.
2. Pam whistled and screeched on her blow horn.
3. Rex told Pam and Mark to be quiet.
4. Pam and Mark sat quietly in the tree house.
5. Rex was angry about the noise.
6. Pam and Mark took no action. They sat still and they were too frightened to do anything at all.
7. Pam and Mark discovered sounds they had never heard before and they saw creatures they had never seen before.
8. Yes, it was important for them to be quiet so that they could see and hear things they had never seen and heard before, and/or so that they would not disturb others.
9. Yes, we know this because he roared at them.
10. Answers will vary. The message from the author may be think of others, don't be self-centred, listen and learn, others have rights.

Unit 10 Tyrannosaurus Rex

1. A favourite dinosaur is the Tyrannosaurus Rex.
2. We are likely to see a Tyrannosaurus Rex in a movie.
3. A Tyrannosaurus Rex is about 13 metres long and about 7 tonnes. (7000 kg)
4. A Tyrannosaurus Rex's legs are so large and strong because they had such a heavy weight to carry. (7 tonnes)
5. They did not need large arms but they did have strong arms so that they could hold onto their prey so that it did not get away.
6. The Tyrannosaurus Rex had a big head and big teeth so it could crush the bones of its prey and other dinosaurs.
7. Other dinosaurs would run away from the Tyrannosaurus Rex because it was so large, it looked fierce and its strong arms and teeth could catch them and crush them easily. (Students may write only parts of this response to be correct.)
8. Scientists found out about the Tyrannosaurus Rex's head and teeth from studying its bones. (Note the answer does not appear in the text, students must infer this from what they know and from what they read.)
9. We do not know everything because there are no dinosaurs alive today and there are no records in existence that document their existence. We must rely on what scientists and archaeologists can gather from their investigations.
10. Answers will vary. People are fascinated by dinosaurs for many reasons. Their size, the unknown, and the fact that they appear in movies causes us to be inquisitive about them.

Unit 11 Vocabulary 3

1. a) to b) do c) only d) like e) are f) many g) words h) we i) its j) or
2. Adult to check.

Unit 12 Quick Quiz 3

1. a) screeched: high pitched squeal

   b) growled: low deep noise showing warning

   c) hummed: noise made while lips kept together

   d) noisier: louder than another

   e) whistled: sound made by blowing through lips
2. **Dinosaurs** are the most interesting **creatures** to have ever walked the Earth. My two **favourite** movies are ***Jurassic** Park* and *Night at the **Museum***. They both have dinosaurs in them and they are both scary. The thing that I like the most about dinosaurs is that they were so large and scary. I can not imagine being alive on the planet at the same time as they were alive. I would be scared!

Unit 13 A Lizard's Day

1. The four stages are early morning, late morning, afternoon and night.
2. In the first stage, a lizard warms itself in the sun before going hunting.
3. In the second stage, it hunts to catch insects and small animals.
4. In the third stage, the lizard rests in the sun to digest its food and in the fourth stage, it finds a safe place to sleep.
5. A lizard is most active in the second stage of its day, when hunting.
6. A lizard is most restful at night when it sleeps. (Some students may say the afternoon, as it is resting after having eaten. Adults can decide to accept this answer, depending on the explanation given.)

ANSWERS

7. It chooses this time of day because its body is warm and it can move quickly. (Note the similarity with our bodies – we warm up before exercise so that we can perform better.)
8. The lizard chooses this time of day because it is cold and the lizard is cold, so it cannot be so active. Students may also mention that the lizard's prey are not available to prey upon.
9. The early morning would be best while it is resting in the sun and is only moving slowly.
10. Yes, because it must catch its own food to survive and can only hunt when its blood has warmed enough for it to move quickly to catch prey. Students may also mention that the lizard, while laying in the sun to warm up, could be easy prey.

Unit 14 Your Heart

1. Your heart could be described as an engine.
2. Your body needs a heart and blood to make it go.
3. The heart muscle pumps blood around the body. (Which contains oxygen and nutrients)
4. Our body needs oxygen and nutrients to make it work.
5. Our heart beats faster when we exercise because the body needs more oxygen and nutrients to do the extra work.
6. Our heart beats slower when we are not exercising because our body does not need as many nutrients or as much oxygen when we are not exercising.
7. Our heart still needs to work at night because there are parts of our body that still work while we are asleep! Some students may say simply that without the heart working, we would be dead. Accept any logical answer.
8. Answers may vary. The heart is the most important part of our body because it is like the body's engine.
9. A doctor always listens to a person's heart because it is the engine of the body, so the doctor must make sure it is working properly.
10. Our heart is perhaps placed here so that the ribs can help to **protect** the heart from external damage. Protection is the key concept here.

Unit 15 Vocabulary 4

Adult to review and check correct spelling.

Unit 16 Quick Quiz 4

1. Adult to check words have been written inside the snail's shell and on the snail trail correctly.
2. a) heart b) oxygen c) blood d) insects e) lizard f) hunt

Unit 17 Polar Bears

1. The world's largest carnivores are polar bears.
2. Polar bears live on ice floes in the Arctic.
3. Polar bears are in danger because of global warming.
4. The two layers of fur and the thick layer of blubber protect polar bears from the cold.
5. Camouflage (its ability to blend in with the colour of the snow) helps the polar bear hunt prey as it cannot be seen easily. (Students may only articulate part of this answer to be correct)
6. Polar bears eat seals, birds, fish and small whales. (Students may only list one or more of these to be correct)
7. The polar bear's large paws act like paddles and help it move through the water.
8. Answers may vary. Camouflage, because this helps it hunt for food. Its large paws, as they help it travel around so that it can find prey. Its size and ferocity, which make it a killing machine! (Student like to articulate a dominant species)
9. Answers will vary. Global warming is bad for the bears because their home is melting, which means there is less space for them to live and less space for their prey to live.
10. Answers will vary. Adult to review and discuss with student.

Unit 18 The Moon

1. The Moon is about 4½ billion years old.
2. It takes about 27.3 days for the Moon to go around the Earth.
3. The Moon is very hot during the day, about 107°C.
4. The Moon is very cold during the night, about -153°C.
5. The journey for the first man to land on the Moon took about 13 hours.
6. Astronauts need special suits on the Moon to keep them on the ground because there is no gravity.
7. They would notice that there is no air, water or life on the Moon.
8. Crescent, quarter, full
9. Answers may vary. Humans may be interested in landing on the Moon because they have not been there; because they have learned about it but have never seen it for themselves; or because they see it in movies and imagine what it would be like. Other answers may be acceptable.
10. Answers will vary.

Unit 19 Vocabulary 5

Adult to review.

ANSWERS

Unit 20 Quick Quiz 5

1. Adult to review.

2.

Word	Meaning
carnivores	meat eating
Arctic	far north of the planet
prey	hunted to eat
blubber	layer of fat
camouflage	coloured to blend in with the environment, to hide
crescent	a curved shape, wide in the middle and pointed at the ends
quarter	one of four parts
rocket	vehicle to travel in space
gravity	the force that causes objects to fall
astronaut	person who travels in space

Test 1 Comprehension
2, 4, 3, 5, 1

Test 2 Comprehension
4, 1, 3, 2

Test 3 High-Frequency Words
Use the numbered high-frequency word cards to check the correct answers.